I0781426

Virginia Woolf:
The Life and Legacy of a Literary Modernist

Born Adeline Virginia Stephen on January 25, 1882, Virginia Woolf came into the world during a time of social and intellectual transformation. Her father, Sir Leslie Stephen, was an influential literary critic, historian, and editor of the Dictionary of National Biography, while her mother, Julia Duckworth Stephen, came from a lineage of beauty and grace, having served as a model for Pre-Raphaelite artists. The Stephen family's roots in Victorian intellectual society deeply influenced Virginia's formative years, instilling in her an early awareness of culture, art, and literature. However, it was also a household marred by internal struggles and repressive social expectations.

Tragedy struck Virginia Woolf early. She was only 13 when her mother died suddenly in 1895, plunging her into profound grief that would shadow her life. This loss, followed by the death of her half-sister Stella two years later, led to her first major mental breakdown, creating a fragile emotional foundation that she would carry throughout her life. These early experiences shaped her sensitivity to loss and mortality, underscoring her later literary explorations of mental illness and the complex inner lives of her characters.

Education and Early Literary Development (1895–1904)

The Stephen household was an inspiring environment for young Virginia, where she and her siblings had full access to their father's vast

library. Surrounded by books, art, and philosophy, Virginia was encouraged to read widely, from classic to contemporary works, fueling her intellectual curiosity. Unlike her brothers, who went on to college, Virginia was educated at home, reflecting the educational limitations women faced at the time. Nonetheless, she became a diligent self-educator, immersing herself in Shakespeare, Greek classics, and Victorian novels—interests that would profoundly shape her writing. Later, she observed that her self-guided learning left her better educated than many contemporaries who had formally studied at Cambridge.

After her father's death in 1904, Virginia's life changed dramatically. She and her siblings moved to the vibrant Bloomsbury district in London, seeking independence from their family's Victorian restraints. Here, freed from the confines of the Stephen household, Virginia began to cultivate her own identity. She soon transformed her grief and anxiety into a formidable literary ambition, writing essays, diaries, and short stories that foreshadowed her later mastery of the modernist novel.

The Bloomsbury Group and the Emergence of Woolf's Voice (1904–1912)

In Bloomsbury, Virginia and her siblings began hosting regular gatherings with some of the era's most progressive thinkers, artists, and writers. This circle, which became known as the Bloomsbury Group, included figures such as economist John Maynard Keynes, biographer Lytton Strachey, novelist E.M. Forster, and art critic Clive Bell. The group fostered an atmosphere of freedom and intellectual openness, challenging Victorian norms and embracing a spirit of experimentation. Here, Virginia found the encouragement to push against traditional literary structures and develop her unique narrative style, which focused on the psychological and emotional depths of her characters.

The Bloomsbury Group's influence on Woolf was profound. They questioned the values of the Victorian era, rejecting its repressive attitudes toward sexuality, class, and gender. The group's radical ethos resonated with Virginia's own ideas, allowing her to engage in philosophical discussions that informed her later works. Woolf's early writings during this period, including essays and short stories, reflect the influence of these conversations as she began to experiment with narrative perspectives, time shifts, and the inner monologue style that would become her trademark.

Marriage to Leonard Woolf and Founding of the Hogarth Press (1912–1917)

In 1912, Virginia married Leonard Woolf, a fellow intellectual and writer whom she had met through her Bloomsbury connections. Leonard's background in politics and colonial studies, combined with his intellectual rigor, complemented Virginia's introspective literary style. Though Virginia's mental health remained fragile, Leonard's unwavering support helped her navigate the personal challenges that could have derailed her career. He became Virginia's most dedicated partner, assisting her through recurring mental breakdowns and recognizing the depth of her talent even when she doubted it herself.

In 1917, the couple founded the Hogarth Press from their home, initially using it as a means to publish Virginia's own work without the constraints of a traditional publishing house. The press soon grew into an influential small press, publishing works by T.S. Eliot, Katherine Mansfield, and Sigmund Freud, among others. The Hogarth Press allowed Virginia and Leonard to control the artistic integrity of their publications, providing an outlet for Virginia's own books as well as for the works of other experimental writers of the time. This venture further solidified Virginia's position in the literary world and allowed her the freedom to explore new forms of storytelling.

Formative Themes and Woolf's Early Works

Through her early experiments with form and narrative, Virginia began addressing themes that would come to define her later novels: the fluidity of time, the complexity of memory, and the psychological depth of ordinary experiences. Her debut novel, The Voyage Out (1915), is an early example of Woolf's exploration of identity and self-discovery. The novel follows Rachel Vinrace, a young woman who embarks on a journey to South America, where she encounters various characters that challenge her sheltered worldview. As Rachel navigates love and philosophical questions, Woolf delves into the limitations society places on women, foreshadowing themes that would become central in her later work.

Her early pieces and essays, some of which she published through the Hogarth Press, were characterized by a reflective and sometimes introspective voice that sought to capture the fleeting sensations and emotions of everyday life. Woolf's unique voice was developing, influenced by her surroundings, the philosophical questions posed by her peers, and her own complex inner life.

Virginia Woolf's first major novel, Jacob's Room (1922), marked a pivotal step in her development as a modernist writer. The novel tells the story of Jacob Flanders, a young man whose life is presented through fragmented glimpses rather than a continuous narrative. Loosely based on her brother Thoby, who died in 1906, the novel avoids conventional structure and instead offers impressions of Jacob's experiences, interactions, and eventual fate in World War I. This experimental form received praise for its originality, giving Woolf the confidence to pursue even more ambitious projects. The fragmented style of Jacob's Room laid the foundation for her distinctive narrative approach, which often blurred the lines between past and present, inner thoughts and external events.

Her next novel, Mrs Dalloway (1925), remains one of her most celebrated works. Set over the course of a single day in post-World War I London, the novel follows Clarissa Dalloway as she prepares to host an evening party. Interwoven with her story is that of Septimus Warren Smith, a war veteran suffering from severe trauma. Through the experiences of Clarissa and Septimus, Woolf explores themes of trauma, identity, and societal expectations. Using a stream-of-consciousness technique, Woolf reveals the inner worlds of her characters, transforming the seemingly mundane into profound moments of insight. The novel's innovative style and psychological depth cemented Woolf's reputation as a central figure in modernist literature, captivating readers and critics alike.

Following the success of Mrs Dalloway, Woolf published To the Lighthouse (1927), often considered her finest work. Set on the Isle of Skye, the novel centers around the Ramsay family and their visits to their summer home, focusing on Mrs. Ramsay's efforts to maintain unity within her family. As they plan a long-anticipated trip to the lighthouse, Woolf explores themes of memory, loss, and the passage of time. This semi-autobiographical novel reflects Woolf's own family experiences and the lasting impact of her mother's death. The fluid structure of To the Lighthouse and its introspective style further solidified Woolf's place among literary giants, with its sensitive portrayal of family dynamics and the complexities of human relationships resonating widely.

Social and Feminist Developments in Woolf's Works (1928–1931)

Virginia Woolf's Orlando (1928) marks a groundbreaking exploration of gender and identity, challenging traditional perspectives on both. The novel follows its protagonist across centuries, during which they transform between genders, symbolizing the fluidity of self. Through this inventive narrative, Woolf critiques the constraints of societal gender roles and probes into the complexities of identity, establishing Orlando as a pioneering work in feminist literature. This novel showcases Woolf's commitment to examining the intersections of gender, art, and social norms, solidifying her role as a leading voice in feminist thought.

Building on the themes introduced in Orlando, her landmark work, A Room of One's Own (1929), emerged from a series of lectures she delivered on "Women and Fiction." This extended essay, blending fiction and polemic, explores the systemic barriers women face in the literary world. Woolf famously argues that a woman needs both financial independence and personal space—symbolized by "a room of one's own"—to create literature or pursue any artistic endeavor. Through the fictional story of Shakespeare's imagined sister Judith, Woolf illustrates how societal constraints have historically silenced women's voices and stifled their potential. A Room of One's Own is now regarded as one of the foundational texts in feminist literature, profoundly shaping feminist discourse by highlighting the essential resources and freedoms necessary for women to achieve equality.

Continuing to build on the momentum of her feminist thought, Woolf published The Waves (1931), her most experimental novel. Structured as a series of soliloquies by six central characters—Bernard, Susan, Rhoda, Neville, Jinny, and Louis—the novel follows each character from childhood through adulthood, revealing their evolving relationships, identities, and inner struggles. Through a symphony of voices, The Waves transcends individual consciousness to explore the collective human experience, blurring the boundaries between each character's thoughts and emotions. The novel's poetic style and its fluid treatment of time reflect Woolf's fascination with interconnectedness and the universality of human experience. While challenging for some readers, The Waves demonstrated Woolf's bold commitment to narrative innovation and remains one of her most ambitious works.

Later Works and Public Persona (1932–1941)

In the years following The Waves, Woolf continued to publish both novels and essays, each marked by her unique insight and introspection. In The Years (1937), a sweeping multi-generational novel, Woolf delves into the lives of the Pargiter family across several decades. The story follows them through pivotal moments in British history, from the late Victorian era to the 1930s, portraying how personal and family dynamics are shaped by societal changes. Woolf uses the novel to reflect on themes of memory, the effects of time, and the changing roles of women, weaving together family narratives with broader social commentary on British life.

With Three Guineas (1938), Woolf turned her attention more directly to social and political issues, especially the intersections of patriarchy and militarism. Structured as a series of letters, the book responds to a question about how to prevent war, ultimately becoming a polemic against the patriarchal structures that foster inequality and oppression. Woolf argues for social reform, gender equality, and the dismantling of hierarchies that sustain war and injustice. Through her critique of institutions like the military and higher education, Three Guineas addresses the broader social inequalities of her era, further cementing Woolf's reputation as a feminist thinker and social critic.

Personal Life, Struggles, and Final Days

Throughout her life, Woolf struggled with recurrent episodes of depression and mental illness, which intensified following traumatic family losses. The death of her mother when Woolf

was just thirteen marked her first severe depressive episode. This was soon followed by the loss of her half-sister Stella, leading to further psychological turmoil. When her father, Leslie Stephen, died in 1904, Woolf's grief triggered another severe breakdown, during which she reportedly attempted to jump out of a window, underscoring the profound impact of these early losses on her mental health.

A significant influence on Woolf's life was Vita Sackville-West, a fellow writer and member of the Bloomsbury Group with whom she shared an intense friendship and romantic bond. Sackville-West was a continual source of inspiration and connection for Woolf, inspiring the character of Orlando, whose life transcends time and the boundaries of gender. Through Orlando, Woolf playfully reflects their shared ideals of identity's fluid nature and deep connection beyond societal expectations. Her relationship with Sackville-West enriched Woolf's personal and creative life, providing companionship and intellectual rapport she deeply valued.

As she advanced in her career, Woolf faced mounting psychological stress. The horrors of World War I, which left a generation scarred, and the looming threat of World War II weighed heavily on her mind. The demands of her writing, combined with these traumas, made it increasingly difficult for her to maintain stability. A particular disappointment came with the lackluster reception of Roger Fry's biography, which she had hoped would be a celebration of her friend's contributions to the art world. Additionally, her husband Leonard Woolf joining the Home Guard upset her pacifist nature,

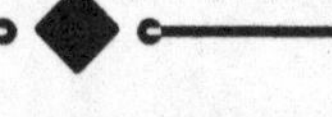

further complicating her emotional landscape. Although Leonard provided love and support, and her work offered some solace, her battles with mental illness persisted throughout her life, casting a shadow over even her most successful years.

On March 28, 1941, Woolf left a tender and heartbreaking note for Leonard, thanking him for the life they shared and expressing her love and gratitude. Feeling increasingly overcome by despair and fearing that her mental health struggles were becoming a burden, she walked to the River Ouse near her home in Sussex, placed stones in her pockets, and waded into the water, ending her life.

Legacy and Influence

Woolf's death marked the loss of one of the most visionary voices of the 20th century. Her novels and essays continue to resonate for their groundbreaking approach to narrative form, their exploration of human consciousness, and their fearless examination of the social and psychological constraints faced by women. A Room of One's Own remains foundational in feminist literature, advocating for women's independence and creative freedom, while Mrs. Dalloway and To the Lighthouse continue to influence writers and readers with their deep psychological insight and stream-of-consciousness style.

Beyond literature, Woolf's legacy extends into feminist discourse and mental health awareness, highlighting the resilience and vulnerability of those who confront mental illness. Her work invites readers to question the boundaries of

identity, society, and creative freedom, and her life and writings have inspired countless individuals to explore and embrace the complexities of human experience. Woolf's contributions to modernism and her advocacy for women's rights remain essential, ensuring her place as a towering figure in both literature and social thought.

~ ~ ~

Following this exploration of Virginia Woolf's life, we turn to her words—insightful, daring, and timeless. The quotes in this collection, drawn from her novels, essays, and letters, showcase her deep sensitivity to human nature, her candid reflections on mental struggles, and her innovative approach to writing. Woolf's voice resonates powerfully, providing readers with a glimpse into her mind and the unique perspective that established her as one of the most influential writers of her time.

We do not know our own
souls, let alone the souls
of others. Human beings do
not go hand in hand the
whole stretch of the way.
There is a virgin forest
in each; a snowfield where
even the print of birds'
feet is unknown.
Here we go alone, and like
it better so. Always to have
sympathy, always to be
accompanied, always to be
understood would be
intolerable.

('On Being Ill')

Nothing can be more arrogant, though nothing is commoner, than to assume that of Gods there is only one, and of religions none but the speaker's.

('Orlando')

If people are highly successful in their professions they lose their sense. Sight goes. They have no time to look at pictures. Sound goes. They have no time to listen to music. Speech goes. They have no time for conversation. Humanity goes. Money making becomes so important that they must work by night as well as by day. Health goes. And so competitive do they become that they will not share their work with others though they have more themselves. What then remains of a human being who has lost sight, sound, and sense of proportion? Only a cripple in a cave.

('Three Guineas')

Better was it to go
unknown and leave
behind you an arch, a
potting shed, a wall
where peaches ripen,
than to burn like a
meteor and leave no
dust.

('Orlando')

"I want to write a
novel about Silence,"
he said; "the things
people don't say."

('The Voyage Out')

What is a woman?
I assure you, I do not
know ... I do not
believe that anybody
can know until she
has expressed herself
in all the arts and
professions open to
human skill.

('Professions for Women')

Until we can
comprehend the
beguiling beauty of
a single flower, we
are woefully unable
to grasp the meaning
and potential of
life itself.

At last she shut the book sharply, lay back, and drew a deep breath, expressive of the wonder which always marks the transition from the imaginary world to the real world.

('The Voyage Out')

With twice his wits,
she had to see things
through his eyes --
one of the tragedies
of married life.

('Mrs. Dalloway')

It is in our idleness,
in our dreams, that
the submerged truth
sometimes comes to
the top.

('A Room of One's Own')

It is worth mentioning,
for future reference,
that the creative power
which bubbles so
pleasantly in beginning
a new book quiets down
after a time, and one
goes on more steadily.
Doubts creep in. Then
one becomes resigned.
Determination not to
give in, and the sense of
an impending shape keep
one at it more than
anything.

('A Writer's Diary')

As a woman I have no
country. As a woman
my country is the
whole world.

('Three Guineas')

If you do not tell the
truth about yourself
you cannot tell it
about other people.

('The Leaning Tower')

How much better is
silence; the coffee cup,
the table. How much
better to sit by myself
like the solitary sea-
bird that opens its
wings on the stake. Let
me sit here for ever
with bare things, this
coffee cup, this knife,
this fork, things in
themselves, myself
being myself.

('The Waves')

Incessant company is
as bad as solitary
confinement.

('A Writer's Diary')

So the days pass, and I
ask myself whether
one is not hypnotized,
as a child by a silver
globe, by life, and
whether this is
living.

('A Writer's Diary')

We all indulge in the
strange, pleasant
process called
thinking, but when it
comes to saying, even
to someone opposite,
what we think, then
how little we are
able to convey! The
phantom is through
the mind and out of
the window before we
can lay salt on.

(from the essay "Montaigne"
in The Common Reader)

It seemed ... such nonsense -- inventing differences, when people, heaven knows, were different enough without that.

('To the Lighthouse')

The profound difference that divides the human race is a question of bait — whether to fish with worms or not.

('The Moment')

My own brain is to me the most unaccountable of machinery – always buzzing, humming, soaring roaring diving, and then buried in mud. And why? What's this passion for?

('The Letters of Virginia Woolf')

You would get longer livelier and more frequent letters from me, if it weren't for the Christian religion. How that bell tolling at the end of the garden, dum dum, dum dum, annoys me! Why is Christianity so insistent and so sad?

('The Letters of Virginia Woolf')

The immense success of our life is, I think, that our treasure is hid away; or rather in such common things that nothing can touch it.

('The Diary of Virginia Woolf')

The root of things, what they were all afraid of saying, was that happiness is dirt cheap. You can have it for nothing.

('A Haunted House And Other Short Stories')

Illusions are to the soul what atmosphere is to the earth. Roll up that tender air and the plant dies, the colour fades...By the truth we are undone. Life is a dream. 'Tis waking that kills us. He who robs us of our dreams robs us of our life.

('Orlando')

But how entirely I live
in my imagination;
how completely depend
upon spurts of thought,
coming as I walk, as I
sit; things churning
up in my mind and so
making a perpetual
pageant, which is to be
my happiness.

('A Writer's Diary')

But he could not taste,
he could not feel. In the
teashop among the tables
and the chattering
waiters the appalling
fear came over him- he
could not feel. He could
reason; he could read,
Dante for example, quite
easily...he could add up
his bill; his brain was
perfect; it must be the
fault of the world then-
that he could not feel.

('Mrs. Dalloway')

To be caught happy in a world of misery was for an honest man the most despicable of crimes.

('To the Lighthouse')

There is the strange power we have of changing facts by the force of the imagination.

('The Common Reader')

Masterpieces are not single and solitary births; they are the outcome of many years of thinking in common, of thinking by the body of the people, so that the experience of the mass is behind the single voice.

('A Room of One's Own')

The man who is aware of
himself is henceforward
independent, and he is
never bored, and life is
only too short, and he is
steeped through and
through with a profound
yet temperate happiness.
He alone lives, while other
people, slaves of ceremony,
let life slip past them in a
kind of dream.

('The Common Reader')

What does the
brain matter
compared with
the heart?

('Mrs. Dalloway')

I feel so intensely the
delights of shutting
oneself up in a little
world of one's own,
with pictures and
music and everything
beautiful.

('The Voyage Out')

What greater delight and wonder can there be than to leave the straight lines of personality and deviate into these footpaths that lead beneath brambles and thick tree trunks into the heart of the forest where live those wild beasts, our fellow men? That is true: to escape is the greatest of pleasures; street haunting in winter the greatest of adventures.

('The Death of the Moth: and other essays')

How are we to account for the strange human craving for the pleasure of feeling afraid which is so much involved in our love of ghost stories?

('The Essays of Virginia Woolf')

War is a man's game...
the killing machine
has a gender and it is
male.

('Three Guineas')

It was jealousy that
was at the bottom of
it – jealousy which
survives every other
passion of mankind.

('Mrs. Dalloway')

There must be another life,
she thought, sinking back
into her chair, exasperated.
Not in dreams; but here and
now, in this room, with
living people. She felt as
if she were standing on the
edge of a precipice with her
hair blown back; she was
about to grasp something
that just evaded her. There
must be another life, here
and now, she repeated. This
is too short, too broken. We
know nothing, even about
ourselves.

('The Years')

A woman must have
money and a room of
her own if she is to
write fiction.

('A Room of One's Own')

The extraordinary
woman depends on the
ordinary woman.

('Granite and Rainbow')

I read some history: it is suddenly all alive, branching forwards & backwards & connected with every kind of thing that seemed entirely remote before. I seem to feel Napoleons influence on our quiet evening in the garden for instance — I think I see for a moment how our minds are all threaded together — how any live mind today is of the very same stuff as Plato's & Euripides. It is only a continuation & development of the same thing. It is this common mind that binds the whole world together;
& all the world is mind.

('The Diary of Virginia Woolf')

A whole lifetime was too
short to bring out, the
full flavour; to extract
every ounce of pleasure,
every shade of meaning.

But nothing is so strange
when one is in love (and
what was this except
being in love?) as the
complete indifference
of other people.

Walden - all his books,
indeed - are packed with
subtle, conflicting, and very
fruitful discoveries. They
are not written to prove
something in the end. They
are written as the Indians
turn down twigs to mark their
path through the forest.
He cuts his way through life
as if no one had ever taken
that road before, leaving
these signs for those who
come after, should they care
to see which way he went.

(speaking of Henry David Thoreau)

The human frame being
what it is, heart, body
and brain all mixed
together, and not
contained in separate
compartments as they
will be no doubt in
another million years,
a good dinner is of
great importance to
good talk. One cannot
think well, love well,
sleep well, if one has
not dined well.

('A Room of One's Own')

Madness is terrific I can assure you, and not to be sniffed at; and in its lava I still find most of the things I write about. It shoots out of one everything shaped, final, not in mere driblets, as sanity does.

('The Letters of Virginia Woolf')

When an arguer argues
dispassionately
he thinks only
of the argument.

('A Room of One's Own')

My notion's to think
of the human beings
first and let the
abstract ideas take
care of themselves.

('The Voyage Out')

The truth is ... that
human beings have
neither kindness,
nor faith, nor charity
beyond what serves to
increase the pleasure
of the moment. They
hunt in packs. Their
packs scour the desert
and vanish screaming
into the wilderness.

('Mrs. Dalloway')

She dares me to pour
myself out like a
living waterfall.
She dares me to enter
the soul that is more
than my own; she
extinguishes fear in
mere seconds. She
lets light come
through.

('from a diary entry dated 19
February 1925')

The mind must be
allowed to settle
undisturbed over the
object in order to
secrete the pearl.

('The Diary of Virginia Woolf')

No need to hurry.
No need to sparkle.
No need to be anybody
but oneself.

('A Room of One's Own')

For now she need not think of anybody. She could be herself, by herself. And that was what now she often felt the need of - to think; well not even to think. To be silent; to be alone. All the being and the doing, expansive, glittering, vocal, evaporated; and one shrunk, with a sense of solemnity, to being oneself, a wedge-shaped core of darkness, something invisible to others... and this self having shed its attachments was free for the strangest adventures.

('To the Lighthouse')

Different though
the sexes are, they
intermix. In every
human being a
vacillation from
one sex to the other
takes place, and
often it is only the
clothes that keep
the male or female
likeness.

('Orlando')

I can only note that
the past is beautiful
because one never
realises an emotion at
the time. It expands
later, and thus we
don't have complete
emotions about the
present, only about
the past.

('The Diary of Virginia Woolf')

A self that goes on
changing is a self
that goes on living.

My mind works in
idleness. To do
nothing is often my
most profitable way.

('The Diary of Virginia Woolf')

Beauty had this penalty
-- it came too readily,
came too completely. It
stilled life -- froze it.
One forgot the little
agitations; the flush,
the pallor, some queer
distortion, some light or
shadow, which made the
face unrecognisable for
a moment and yet added a
quality one saw for ever
after. It was simpler to
smooth that all out under
the cover of beauty.

('To the Lighthouse')

The most important
thing is not to think
very much about
oneself. To investigate
candidly the charge;
but not fussily, not
very anxiously. On no
account to retaliate by
going to the other
extreme — thinking
too much.

('A Writer's Diary')

To write weekly, to write
daily, to write shortly,
to write for busy people
catching trains in the
morning or for tired
people coming home
in the evening, is a
heartbreaking task
for men who know good
writing from bad. They
do it, but instinctively
draw out of harm's way
anything precious that
might be damaged by
contact with the public,
or anything sharp that
might irritate its skin.

('The Essays of Virginia Woolf')

The mind which is most
capable of receiving
impressions is very
often the least capable
of drawing conclusions.

('The Common Reader')

Why, he wondered, did
people who had been
asleep always want to
make out that they were
extremely wide-awake?

('The Years')

O how blessed it
would be never to
marry, or grow old;
but to spend one's
life innocently and
indifferently among
the trees and rivers
which alone can
keep one cool and
childlike in the
midst of the troubles
of the world!

('The Complete Shorter Fiction of
Virginia Woolf')

What I like, or one of
the things I like, about
motoring is the sense it
gives one of lighting
accidentally, like a
voyager who touches
another planet with the
tip of his toe, upon
scenes which would have
gone on, have always
gone on, will go on,
unrecorded, save for
this chance glimpse.
Then it seems to me I am
allowed to see the heart
of the world uncovered
for a moment.

('The Diary of Virginia Woolf')

The compensation of
growing old ... was
simply this; that the
passion remains as
strong as ever, but one
has gained -- at last!
-- the power which
adds the supreme
flavour to existence
-- the power of taking
hold of experience,
of turning it round,
slowly, in the light.

('Mrs. Dalloway')

Style is a very simple
matter; it is all
rhythm. Once you get
that, you can't use the
wrong words...Now this
is very profound, what
rhythm is, and goes far
deeper than any words.
A sight, an emotion,
creates this wave in
the mind, long before
it makes words to fit
it.

('Selected Letters')

Time, unfortunately, though it makes animals and vegetables bloom and fade with amazing punctuality, has no such simple effect upon the mind of man...An hour, once it lodges in the queer element of the human spirit, may be stretched to fifty or a hundred times its clock length; on the other hand, an hour may be accurately represented on the timepiece of the mind by one second. This extraordinary discrepancy between time on the clock and time in the mind is less known than it should be and deserves fuller investigation.

('Orlando')

The beauty of the world
which is so soon to
perish, has two edges,
one of laughter, one of
anguish, cutting the
heart asunder.

('A Room of One's Own')

We live in constant
danger of coming
apart. The mystery of
why we do not always
come apart is the
animating tension
of all art.

The only advice ...
that one person can
give another about
reading is to take no
advice, to follow your
own instincts, to use
your own reason, to
come to your own
conclusions.

('The Second Common Reader')

Second hand books are
wild books, homeless
books; they have come
together in vast
flocks of variegated
feather, and have a
charm which the
domesticated volumes
of the library lack.

('Street Haunting')

At the age of thirty, or
thereabouts, this young
Nobleman had not only had
every experience that life
has to offer, but had seen
the worthlessness of them
all. Love and ambition,
women and poets were all
equally vain. Literature
was a farce...Two things
alone remained to him in
which he now put any trust:
dogs and nature; an elk-
hound and a rose bush. The
world, in all its variety,
life in all its complexity,
had shrunk to that. Dogs and
a bush were the whole of it.

('Orlando')

The transaction
between a writer and
the spirit of the age
is one of infinite
delicacy, and upon a
nice arrangement
between the two the
whole fortune of his
works depend.

('Orlando')

A sort of transaction
went on between them,
in which she was on
one side, and life was
on another, and she
was always trying to
get the better of it,
as it was of her.

('To the Lighthouse')

Life, from being made up of little separate incidents which one lived one by one, became curled and whole like a wave which bore one up with it and threw one down with it, there, with a dash on the beach.

('To the Lighthouse')

Beyond the difficulty of communicating oneself, there is the supreme difficulty of being oneself. This soul, or life within us, by no means agrees with the life outside us. If one has the courage to ask her what she thinks, she is always saying the very opposite to what other people say.

(from the essay "Montaigne" in The Common Reader)

Doesn't one always
think of the past, in
a garden with men and
women lying under
the trees? Aren't they
one's past, all that
remains of it, those
men and women, those
ghosts lying under
the trees... one's
happiness, one's
reality?

('Monday or Tuesday')

Let us simmer over our incalculable cauldron, our enthralling confusion, our hotchpotch of impulses, our perpetual miracle – for the soul throws up wonders every second. Movement and change are the essence of our being; rigidity is death; conformity is death; let us say what comes into our heads, repeat ourselves, contradict ourselves, fling out the wildest nonsense, and follow the most fantastic fancies without caring what the world does or thinks or says. For nothing matters except life.

(from the essay "Montaigne"
in The Common Reader)

I thought how
unpleasant it is to be
locked out; and I
thought how it is
worse, perhaps, to be
locked in.

('A Room of One's Own')

One likes people much
better when they're
battered down by a
prodigious siege of
misfortune than when
they triumph.

('from a diary entry dated 13
August 1921')

To pursue truth with
such astonishing lack
of consideration for
other people's feelings,
to rend the thin veils
of civilisation so
wantonly, so brutally,
was to her so horrible
an outrage of human
decency that, without
replying, dazed and
blinded, she bent her
head..there was nothing
to be said.

('To the Lighthouse')

To read a novel
is a difficult and
complex art. You must
be capable not only
of great fineness of
perception, but of
great boldness of
imagination.

('The Second Common Reader')

Let us record the atoms
as they fall upon the
mind in the order in
which they fall, let
us trace the pattern,
however disconnected
and incoherent in
appearance, which each
sight or incident scores
upon the consciousness.
Let us not take it for
granted that life exists
more fully in what is
commonly thought big
than in what is commonly
thought small.

('The Common Reader')

The indifference of the world which Keats and Flaubert and other men of genius have found so hard to bear was in her case [the woman writer's] not indifference but hostility. The world did not say to her as it said to them, Write if you choose; it makes no difference to me. The world said with a guffaw, Write? What's the good of your writing?

('A Room of One's Own')

Friendships,
even the best of them,
are frail things.
One drifts apart.

('To the Lighthouse')

Let it be fact, one feels,
or let it be fiction;
the imagination will
not serve under two
masters simultaneously.

('Selected Essays')

But what a little I
can get down into
my pen of what is so
vivid to my eyes,
and not only to my
eyes; also to some
nervous fibre, or
fanlike membrane
in my species.

('A Writer's Diary')

Really I don't like human nature unless all candied over with art.

('The Diary of Virginia Woolf')

Facts must be manipulated; some must be brightened; others shaded; yet, in the process, they must never lose their integrity.

('The New Biography')

We are cut, we
are fallen. We are
become part of that
unfeeling universe
that sleeps when we
are at our quickest
and burns red when
we lie asleep.

('The Waves')

Habits and customs
are a convenience
devised for the
support of timid
natures who dare
not allow their
souls free play.

('The Common Reader')

I like people to be
unhappy because I
like them to have
souls.

('Selected Letters')

That is the quality
which dance music has —
no other: it stirs some
barbaric instinct —
lulled asleep in our
sober lives — you
forget centuries of
civilization in a
second, & yield to that
strange passion which
sends you madly
whirling round the
room...

('A Dance at Queen's Gate')

Growing up is losing some illusions, in order to acquire others.

('Orlando')

I always had the deepest affection for people who carried sublime tears in their silences.

('The Diary of Virginia Woolf')

While fame impedes and
constricts, obscurity
wraps about a man like a
mist; obscurity is dark,
ample, and free;
obscurity lets the mind
take its way unimpeded.
Over the obscure man is
poured the merciful
suffusion of darkness.
None knows where he
goes or comes. He may
seek the truth and speak
it; he alone is free;
he alone is truthful,
he alone is at peace.

('Orlando')

Mental fight means
thinking against the
current, not with it.
It is our business to
puncture gas bags and
discover the seeds of
truth.

('Thoughts on Peace
in an Air Raid')

The eyes of others
our prisons; their
thoughts our cages.

('An Unwritten Novel')

To follow her thought
was like following a
voice which speaks too
quickly to be taken
down by one's pencil,
and the voice was her
own voice saying
without prompting
undeniable,
everlasting,
contradictory
things.

('To the Lighthouse')

Perhaps a mind that
is purely masculine
cannot create, any
more than a mind that
is purely feminine....
It is fatal to be a man
or woman pure and
simple; one must be
woman-manly or man-
womanly.

('A Room of One's Own')

I will not be "famous,"
"great." I will go on
adventuring, changing,
opening my mind and
my eyes, refusing to be
stamped and stereotyped.
The thing is to free one's
self: to let it find its
dimensions, not be
impeded.

('A Writer's Diary')

Night had come—
night that she loved
of all times, night in
which the reflections
in the dark pool of
the mind shine more
clearly than by day.

('Orlando')

When, however, one reads
of a witch being ducked,
of a woman possessed by
devils, of a wise woman
selling herbs, or even a
very remarkable man who
had a mother, then I
think we are on the
track of a lost novelist,
a suppressed poet. . .
indeed, I would venture
to guess that Anon, who
wrote so many poems
without signing them,
was often a woman.

('A Room of One's Own')

In short, if
newspapers were
written by people
whose sole object in
writing was to tell
the truth about
politics and the
truth about art we
should not believe in
war, and we should
believe in art.

('Selected Works of Virginia
Woolf')

Once you begin to take
yourself seriously as a
leader or as a follower,
as a modern or as a
conservative, then you
become a self-conscious,
biting, and scratching
little animal whose
work is not of the
slightest value or
importance to anybody.

('A Letter to a Young Poet')

Women have served all
these centuries as
looking glasses
possessing the power
of reflecting the
figure of man at twice
its natural size.

('A Room of One's Own')

Lock up your libraries
if you like; but there
is no gate, no lock, no
bolt that you can set
upon the freedom of my
mind.

('A Room of One's Own')

One could say nothing to nobody. The urgency of the moment always missed its mark. Words fluttered sideways and struck the object inches too low. Then one gave it up; then the idea sunk back again; then one became like most middle-aged people, cautious, furtive, with wrinkles between the eyes and a look of perpetual apprehension. For how could one express in words these emotions of the body? express that emptiness there?

('To the Lighthouse')

How lovely goodness
is in those who,
stepping lightly,
go smiling through
the world.

('The String Quartet')

But I don't think of
the future, or the
past, I feast on the
moment. This is the
secret of happiness,
but only reached now
in middle age.

('The Diary of Virginia Woolf')

Praise and blame
alike mean nothing.
No, delightful as the
pastime of measuring
may be, it is the most
futile of all
occupations, and to
submit to the decrees
of the measurers the
most servile of
attitudes.

('A Room of One's Own')

In solitude we give
passionate attention
to our lives, to our
memories, to the
details around us.

('A Room of One's Own')

These are the soul's
changes. I don't
believe in ageing.
I believe in forever
altering one's aspect
to the sun. Hence my
optimism.

('A Writer's Diary')

We [women] have borne
and bred and washed
and taught, perhaps
to the age of six or
seven years, the one
thousand six hundred
and twenty-three
million human beings
who are, according to
statistics, at present
in existence, and
that... takes time.

('A Room of One's Own')

How many times have
people used a pen or
paintbrush because
they couldn't pull
the trigger?

('Selected Essays')

Someone has to die in
order that the rest of
us should value life
more.

('from the movie The Hours (2002)
based on the life of Virginia
Woolf')

If one is to deal with
people on a large scale and
say what one thinks, how
can one avoid melancholy?
I don't admit to being
hopeless, though: only the
spectacle is a profoundly
strange one; and as the
current answers don't do,
one has to grope for a new
one, and the process of
discarding the old, when
one is by no means certain
what to put in their place,
is a sad one.

('A Writer's Diary')

Fiction is like a spider's
web, attached ever so lightly
perhaps, but still attached
to life at all four corners.
Often the attachment is
scarcely perceptible;
Shakespeare's plays, for
instance, seem to hang there
complete by themselves. But
when the web is pulled askew,
hooked up at the edge, torn
in the middle, one remembers
that these webs are not spun
in midair by incorporeal
creatures, but are the work
of suffering human beings,
and are attached to the
grossly material things,
like health and money and
the houses we live in.

('A Room of One's Own')

Once conform, once do
what other people do
because they do it,
and a lethargy steals
over all the finer
nerves and faculties
of the soul. She
becomes all outer
show and inward
emptiness; dull,
callous, and
indifferent.

(from the essay "Montaigne"
in The Common Reader)

It is only by putting it into words that I make it whole. This wholeness means that it has lost its power to hurt me; it gives me, perhaps because by doing so I take away the pain, a great delight to put the severed parts together.

('Moments of Being')

And when we are
writing the life of a
woman, we may, it is
agreed, waive our
demand for action,
and substitute love
instead. Love, the
poet has said, is a
woman's whole
existence...

('Orlando')

We may enjoy our room
in the tower, with the
painted walls and the
commodious bookcases,
but down in the garden
there is a man digging
who buried his father
this morning, and it is
he and his like who
live the real life and
speak the real
language.

('The Common Reader')

All great writers have, of course, an atmosphere in which they seem most at their ease and at their best; a mood of the general mind which they interpret and indeed almost discover, so that we come to read them rather for that than for any story or character or scene of separate excellence.

('in a review of Henry James' posthumously published autobiography The Middle Years')